VISIONS

-- VISIONS --

Selected Poems written in Port
Elizabeth in the late 1940's

by
Charles Walter Coulson

E. M. UNDERWOOD, PUBLISHER
Post Office Box 4295
San Leandro, California 94579

Printed in the United States of America
Library of Congress Catalog Card Number 78-65283
International Standard Book Number 0-932410-05-7

Only a few lucky people in this world are given the imagin-ative power that enables them to generate a constant stream of new ideas and images. Even fewer are lucky enough to combine this with a sense of humor and deep human compassion. One of these people is Charles Walter Coulson, teacher, engineer, inventor, traveller, and poet.

Here is a selection of his poetry from a productive period in the immediate post war period in Port Elizabeth, South Africa. An idealism shines through these works, an idealism combined with the hopes and dreams of an immigrant in a new land. His work also recaptures the life and times of a South African city thirty years ago; it was another era, almost a world away now.

These are solid, structured poems meant for the people of the day. They have a mesage behind the humor; it relates to the parish politics and national politics of those times. These poems have stood the test of time, they will always be a delight to read.

Professor H. Quinn

INDEX

I -- Visions

II -- Port Elizabeth

III -- Miscellany

IV -- Cricket and Other Sports

INDEX BY FIRST LINES AND MEMORABLE LINES

A

C

I -- Visions

VISIONS

A race shall rise in Africa,
Far loftier in aim
Than this land ever saw before,
More human yet, I claim;
And it shall spring from this fair soil,
A tolerant, happy breed,
Devoted to its honest toil,
Excelling in good deed;
Combining all the fairest arts
Which they from Europe brought,
With newer, finer counterparts,
That they themselves have wrought.
Of racial hatred no more then,
This country only--first,
Peopled with truer, nobler men,
For progress, peace athirst.
South Africa, thou tortured land,
In wisdom grow, and worth,
Unite, throw off strife's old dead hand,
Forgive--forget--go forth!

UNION DAY

Union Day, the country's emblem.
Where stands Unity to-day?
In this nation that's the problem;
Cleavage has unbounded sway.

Did one party come from Holland,
Honest pioneering folk,
And the other came from England
To escape a tiresome yoke.

Trekking, seeking, working, building,
Overcoming many a foe;
From the forest wrought a living,
Making towns where jungles grew.

Sacrificing life and leisure,
Meeting terror yet awhile,
Ultimately finding pleasure;
Fortune seemed on them to smile.

By their paramount endeavour
Africa was opened wide,
And the White man, now and ever,
In this country could abide.

Room for every Boer and Briton
Could be found in this wide life,
But ere long the land was smitten
By a fratricidal strife.

(continued)

Brother nations, lands of culture,
Protestants from early days,
Fed each other to the vulture,
How came they to evil ways?

Let the past mistakes be buried,
And the future be the aim;
We have argued, fought and worried,
Both sides been too quick to blame.

There are many problems waiting
When we're standing side by side,
But with brother love prevailing,
We could take them in our stride.

Be a Springbok, make it your boast
That this land will make it's way,
Put the country first and foremost;
That's the thought for Union Day.

Now's the time to be United
With a National aim in sight.
Keep the country well supported
On its two legs, left and right.

Union Day, May 31, 1948, South Africa.

RHODESIA'S FUTURE

Of course it matters how you vote,
A right our fathers dearly bought,
So vote--let none dissuade you;
But ere you vote close study make,
To learn what issue is at stake,
Let not the truth evade you!

It's not a case of uncouth race,
That we are called upon to face,
For who's afraid of Kaffirs?
It's federation, Yes! or No!
A stateman's dream, for weal or woe,
A gamble by our gaffers.

The gallant Pioneers set forth,
And trekked into the unknown North,
None will give that denial;
But this is not a Pioneer's move,
It's in a very different groove,

It's politics on trial.

Will copper sell on present lines
Because they're opening three new mines?
Will "money" back the venture?
Where stand white workers in this scheme,
Will fair play always reign supreme,
Have they a certain future?

(continued)

Is federation good or not?
That is the issue to be fought,
So pay no heed to Olley,
He has"black bogy" on the brain,
And pours much good ink down the drain;
His arguments are folly.

Of course it matters how you vote,
Your voter's cross so dearly bought,
A "gun" at your disposal;
So Pioneer the cause of truth,
Forget about "the race uncouth";
Your challenge, my proposal!

WAS THERE ONE *SOUTH AFRICAN?*

There were English, Scots and Hottentots,
Some Hollanders and you-know-what's,
To view the Parliament-ary Parade.
There were Republicans, and Indians,
Staunch O.B.s -- and windy 'uns,
To view the Parliament-ary Parade.
There were Empire-builders, and secret guilders,
Jannies, Johns, Saries and Hildas,
To view the Parliament-ary Parade.
There were Uniteds seeking Unity,
And Nationals with Nationality,
But in the mix-up, near a million
Was there one *South African,*
To view the Parliament-ary Parade?

6

MY WAY

If I had my way in Africa,
Some changes would be wrought,
I'd catch the diamond trafficker,
And make him dig for nought.

Estate agents, who make ascents,
With prices to the heights,
Would live in tents of fabulous rents,
On "most desirable sites."

That dirty dog, the motor hog,
Whose driving turns us grey,
His car would flog 'midst endless fog,
At twenty miles a day.

The affectatious dear young thing,
Whose negative sounds "neau."
Would dwell awhile on Marion Isle,
With Shakespeare for a beau.

The boaster in the beer saloon,
Who blows his trumpet rare,
Would tour the moon in large balloon,
Blown up by his own air.

(continued)

That Shylock queer, the profiteer,
Whose goods are far from good,
I'd put him out to grass a year,
And saw he chewed his cud.

If I had my way in Africa,
Some changes would be wrought,
The people would be happier,
At least, that's what I thought!

THE IMMIGRANT'S DREAM

His breast was bare, his shiny hair
Amingled with the sand;
The immigrant at Humewood lay;
He'd reached the Promised Land.

No more the weary, dreary queue,
No more the ration card,
The fuel shortage out of view,
Life was no longer hard.

The sunshine warm, the murmuring deep,
The playful, soothing breeze,
Soon lulled the immigrant to sleep;
He dreamt -- was ill at ease.

Again he saw his native land,
And shivered, sobbed and sighed,
'Twas Friday night, his bath at hand
Had water -- cold -- inside.

Into the icy bath he leapt
Just like a man possessed,
And gave a gasp as chilling wet
Came swirling o'er his chest.

(continued)

A lifeguard dragged him to his feet,
The crowd's relief was great,
The immigrant was not to meet
A most untimely fate.

His breast was bare, his shiny hair
Was wet -- but joy returned,
For though the tide had caught him fair
Life's tide had also turned.

No more the weary, dreary queue,
No more the ration card.
He dressed; went to a place he knew,
Tea, eggs, ham; nothing barred.

TRIBUTE TO JAN SMUTS

A happy birthday, dear Jan Smuts,
And many more we hope you'll see;
A leader grand of our fair land,
World statesman of celebrity;
Our greatest man despite all ifs and buts --
    Let all toast Smuts.

Out of the fratricidal shame,
Emerged this man with vision fair,
Who wisely planned to make our land
United; strong; loved everywhere;
A mighty task that called for faith and guts --
    Let all toast Smuts.

In time of war he clearly saw
South Africa's true destiny,
He took the stand and placed our land
Alongside of democracy;
See now that here no proud dictator struts --
    Let all toast Smuts.

Prosperity and peace be yours,
And many happy leisure hours
To climb beloved Tafelberg,
And there renew your strength and powers;
A lofty mind that knows no common ruts --
    Let all toast Smuts.

Jan Smuts, eminent South African statesman.

PRINCESS ELIZABETH'S SON

We hail thee, Royal Child,
 We greet thee with felicity,
A long and happy life
 we wish in all sincerity;
A son of noble birth,
 A future man of destiny,
We pray that years of worth
 Shall follow thy nativity.
Combine the ancient lore
 Of thy Hellenic dynasty,
With Britain's modern store
 Of statesmanship and industry,
Blest with Achilles' might;
 A leader like Montgomery;
An Ajax in the fight;
 Churchill's gift of oratory.
The ancient throne still stands,
 Surmounting each vicissitude;
The hub of world-wide lands,
 The Crown with no similitude.

(continued)

A Commonwealth is bound
    By brother-love, not servitude,
The mystic links are sound
    That join the King and multitude.
So, son we wish thee well,
    May years reveal much happiness,
And future stories tell
    Of duty done with diligence;
Here's health unto the boy
    Who's born to Royal eminence,
Thy birth has brought us joy,
    Thy life add joyous evidence!

The future King of England, born in 1948. There had been a Royal visit to Southern Africa just after the War.

THE HUMAN BREED

Do you rise at early day break
    fit and ready for the toil?
Do you labour till your bones ache,
    and your hands and clothing soil?
You are one of Friday's children,
    waiting for the weekly pay.
Other men may make a million;
    simply, you're not made that way.
By your labour you're creating
    something in a world of wealth;
But your share's evaporating --
    stolen with a devil's stealth.
You will never have a penny
    while world statesmen play with power.
Years of building work of many,
    War can shatter in an hour.
For the Powers-that-be are cunning;
    They don't study you and I.
Easily they keep us running
    with some worn-out battle cry.
"Armaments. Oh! you must heed us.
    Ready for the next World War.
We Can't stop it," say the leaders.
    Yet, we've heard it twice before!

On these scatterbrain adventures
    mankind's wealth is poured away.
You are saddled with debentures
    that a lifetime cannot pay.
Try to find some politicians who,
    through goodwill would ensure
Certitude for people's visions
    of a peace that will endure.
There's a smiling, verdant pasture
    waiting for this human breed.
There are avenues of venture where
    the decent ones might lead.
Building house for the masses;
    cheap and clean and wholesome homes.
Better hospitals and buses;
    educate the humble drones.
For the aged every comfort --
    make declining years a treat.
For the crippled ample pensions,
    no more begging in the street.
For the blind some new vocation,
    help them learn a useful trade.

It would ease the situation
    if some simple plans were made.
 For the workers better treatment
    to induce more brains and skill.
Help the mothers, help the teachers
    make our children happier still.
All these benefits afford us
    from the millions spent on War.
They are your election causes
    not the claptrap as of yore.
Were the voters at election,
    matters such as these to heed,
We should have a grand selection,
    Members from the Human Breed.

EXPLOSIONS! Conflagrations!
Excitement at "fire-stations,"
When skies glow bright,
For Guy Fawkes night,
A spark for imaginations.
In Ottowa and Malta,
In Melbourne and Gibralter,
Pianos, tyres,
Are thrown on fires,
Burnt offerings on Guy's altar.
Hearty octogenarians,
Ascetic vegetarians,
Poke each one's ribs,
And let off squibs,
Catherine-wheels please rotarians.
The Russians near the Kremlin,
In apprehension trembling,
Stand well back from
Joe's atom bomb,
A "cracker" he's assembling.
A studious Oriental,
A Frenchman temperamental,
A terrible Turk,
Join in this work,
Universal, monumental.
In atmosphere electric,
Devotees' fever hectic,
They keep alive,
November five,
The Festival Pyrotechnic!

CHRISTMAS EVE

When he was sure the children slept,
Dear Santa to the nursery crept
With loving hands to place the toys,
That mean so much to girls and boys.
Who is this person, now revered,
With long red robe and snow-white beard
Whose gifts to children, rich and poor,
Love, perfect love, reveals once more?
He is a spirit that prevails
At Christmas-time, and never fails
To fold the cloak of human sin,
Revealing human hearts within.

The drunkard scorns his sordid haunt;
The nagging housewife holds her taunt;
The proud unbend, the mighty stoop;
The weak find strength, the outcasts hope;
The selfish give -- lo! it would seem
That men have caught a heavenly gleam,
For sinners all, with saving grace,
Give little children rightful place;
When Santa Claus on his tiptoes
Among the cots so quietly goes,
On Christmas Eve, the path he's trod
Has brought him very near to God.

WAR BEGETS WAR

World of men, where is it heading;
Is it trembling on the brink
Of a Fate we all are dreading?
Now's the time to act and think!

War begets war, conquest kindles
Fires of hatred never quenched.
Hope of Peace enduring dwindles,
Reason from its place is wrenched.

Will conflicting views of nations
Bring the struggle we know well
Quick would shake the world's foundations,
Blasting life and love to hell.

Must it be while statesmen wrangle
Armageddon is let loose;
Common man again to dangle
like a felon on a noose?

Feed the cannon, feed the cannon,
Stop the breach and man the line.
See! the elder statesmen beckon
To a death which they decline.

War was once courageous battle,
Blow for blow and man to man;
Now, behold the human cattle
Sent to slaughter, as to plan.

(continued)

Women cringing, children clinging,
Crawl like beasts to shelters dark.
Is this our idea of bringing
Nobler life? Such madness -- stark!

Men of science, let your morrows
Have a purpose human, clear;
Conquer our besetting sorrows;
Famine; flood; disease and fear.

Statesmen, moderate your rantings,
Drop the stupid parrot cries,
Worried mankind is not wanting
Atom war at any price!

Memories of the recent carnage of the
Second World War were strong.

DUNKIRK, JUNE 4, 1940

On Dunkirk beaches British soldiers lay,
Those agonising, mocking days in June,
When German planes swooped on their disarmed prey,
Who waited in odd groups at every dune.

Three hundred thousand men were gathered there,
Escape, survival from most thoughts had fled,
How empty now must seem each curse or prayer,
Three hundred thousand men as good as dead.

There, just across that narrow neck of sea,
Lay Britain, freedom's outpost, freedom's home,
And dear ones whom we never more would see,
Except, by grace of God, in Kingdom come.

With wistful eye we scanned the seascape o'er,
When, suddenly, the little ships appeared
The sea-dog blood would own no tyrant's power,
Those little ships nor Hun, nor devil feared.

To save or sink in trying was their aim,
While bombs descend, beserk machine-guns spit,
Still closer in the tiny vessels came,
With skill and daring scorning ghastly hit.

(continued)

By hook or crook, or some say heaven's grace,
Describe it by whatever phrase you will,
Most of those men were taken from that place,
Were spirited away to fight on still.

In that proud action Britain's secret lies,
For when around her throat the tyrant grips,
The courage of her people seems to rise,
They calmly save the day with "little ships."

II -- Port Elizabeth

SIGNS OF SUMMER

When balmy breezes blow along Main Street,
At half-gale force and lift us off our feet,
There is an explanation for this treat,
Summer's coming in.

The tranquil ocean woos the Humewood shore,
Invites the bathers to plunge in once more,
Then promptly knocks them flat with angry roar,
Summer's coming in.

A merry lark that takes our breath away,
Is passing near the creek, it 'hums', I say,
And rivals Newton Park on bucket day,
Summer's coming in.

The rare old Korsten timbers creak and sigh,
We wonder why they don't break down and cry,
Where-er you look the dust blows in your eye,
Summer's coming in.

The maidens don their shorts of varied hue,
See! daisies are near white and violets blue,
While others look like they've been up the flue,
Summer's coming in.

From nearby gardens one can smell a rose,
Night-scented stocks of boose a-gurgling flows,
A bottle-tit displays its scarlet nose,
Summer's coming in.

CAN SIR THOMAS TEACH 'EM?

While Sir Thomas Beecham, a chap who can teach 'em
Fine points of the musician's art,
This country is touring, he must be kept roaring
At knowledge some Springbok's impart;
That Beethoven's classics will cure your rheumatics,
And Bach is the voice of a dog,
While Elgar's long marches have flattened his arches,
So Chopin is hacking a log.
Poor Schubert's Unfinished is quickly diminished
With "Why can't he finish it now?
If one mentions Haydn they seek but won't find him,
For Haydn's in hiding -- and how!
Please don't bring up Handel, that will snuff Art's candle,
One handle they turn if they can,
The old organ wheezes, out Blue Danube sneezes,
Last Strauss clutched by poor drowning man.
They don't know Rossini from B Mussolini,
While Mendlesohn's plain meddlesome,
The genius of Delius is bound to sound tedious
When pianos are played with one thumb.
Their musical knowledge was ended at college
When thrilling to Sinatra's trills;
If Sir Thomas Beecham finds he cannot teach 'em
He'll reach 'em a box of his pills!

Sir Thomas Beecham, famous English conductor toured
South Africa in 1948.

NO GRANT FOR MUSIC

"Let's have an orchestra," people said,
"Culture in Port Elizabeth's dead."
Started a fund to further the aim
With what result? Opponents amd blame.

Music won't pay, the rates will increase,"
"Just class distinction," and such like pleas.
Blows aimed to fell enthusiasts low.
Why should these folk oppose Progress so?

Any fond parent sending his child
To be taught music, is reconciled
To paying teachers, seeking no gain
From such a gesture; would it be sane?

Surely, our city needs civic pride,
Counting this cost will impede its stride.
Art, glorious Art shall repay the fee
With souls of men, if not L.S.D.

PATIENCE!

Oh! had I the pen of a Gilbert,
I'd dip it in acid, not ink,
Then start to be curt; the people I'd hurt
Are Opera fans who don't think.

Some came dashing in like the last heat,
The overture's half-done by now;
First stamping their feet, then banging the seat,
They made such a deuce of a row.

The chatter of some brainless females,
Kept Sullivan fighting to win;
Such unending tales -- description, it fails;
The music accompanied their din.

Delightful's my word for the stage show,
'Twas "Patience" as "Patience" should be,
But people who go, should keep quiet, you know;
With patience we'll get them to see!

There was some misbehaviour at the Opera one
Saturday night in September 1947.

27

AT THE PORT ELIZABETH SHOW

The Show inside the Show was fine,
    The audience enraptured sat,
While Wightman plied his snappy line,
And songs and dances went off pat.
The "Can-Can" reached a happy pitch,
    Shades of immortal Offenbach!
Did this "hot" number cause the hitch
    That left the stage turns in the dark?

Two comic ladies were all set,
    And by a "fuse" were funnier made,
They surely will get credit yet,
    For comedy with light and shade.

The most important man in town,
    "Oh, Sparks, dear boy, where have you gone?
Come quickly, get the fuses down,
    The show, the show, must still go on."
When Douglas Catt began to sing,
    Of "Sparkling Eyes" and counsel wise,
I doubt if he could see a thing,
    Although dear Douglas has Catt's eyes!

So let the lights be put to rights,
    Such tragedy inspires the must,
To see light comedy's bright lights
    All blotted out by one small fuse!!

Problems with the lights at the Port Elizabeth Show.

OH! OH! OH! OKLAHOMA!

Oh! what a beautiful morning,
Oh! what a beautiful day,
I bought a ticket for something,
Oh! what a hole in my pay;
When I came out of my coma,
And understood what I'd done,
It was to see Oklahoma,
Greatest show under the sun.

I broke the news nice and quietly;
My wife cried "Heavens above!
Let you go see it -- not likely!
People will say we're in love.
I walk about like a scarecrow,
Don't even get a new hat;
You spend a pound on a stage show --
Go get it back -- and that's flat."

When I went back they regretted,
"No cash refunded, by heck!"
And when I fumed and I fretted
They put me out, on my neck.
Oh! what a horrible bloomer,
Guess what the latest will be,
My wife will see Oklahoma --
And then describe it to me!

The show "Oklahoma" was one of the
biggest successes in South Africa in 1948.

MANY HAPPY RETURNS

What has filled a long-felt need?
Done it very well indeed,
It's the paper you now read,
    The Daily Advertiser.

What brings all the latest news,
Pictures; stories that amuse,
Sports, reports, views and reviews,
    The Daily Advertiser.

What has made the evenings bright,
Bringing in the "daily" light,
And is snapped up with delight,
    The Daily Advertiser.

Light the candle, cut the cake,
Drink its health, make no mistake,
One year old, but wide awake!
    The Daily Advertiser.

The Daily Advertiser, A Port Elizabeth newspaper.

VALENTINE

Ah! mystic day of Valentine,
　　In mundane years of '49,
　　Can it still find a place?
I vow that youths and maids still pine,
Have callow loves as I had mine,
Till longing hearts find one sublime,
　　By fickle Cupid's grace.
My love is like a red, red, rose;
Is really sweet in verse or prose,
　　Let's give romance its fling.
They say, to-day the wild-birds mate,
So it's no time to sit and wait;
Go forth and try your hand with fate,
　　Faint heart ne'er won a thing.
Its love that makes the world go round,
Without it life is empty found,
　　A very dull affair.
Seek one true love and make it thine;
A message that has rung through time,
Is still a fitting Valentine
　　For lovelorn everywhere.

LESS AND LESS

Just two or three decades ago,
The golden sovereign could be found,
And was well worth its face value
Of twenty shillings to the pound;
Alas! the powers that be decreed
That it should leave its well-earned place,
Then gave us paper notes instead,
And made our lives a paper-chase.
The price of things went up sky high,
The cost of living did increase,
And each pound note now lived a lie,
For it was worth a five-bob piece;
This wont to shink still knows no bounds,
And soon it will be seen by many,
A house will cost a million pounds,
The day pound notes are four-a-penny!

ALGOA BAY ARMADA

The shades of night were falling fast
As out of P.E. Harbour passed
A mariner of surly mien,
Who'd been out there since New Year's E'en.
Out in the Bay, Algoa Bay.

His brow was sad, his eyes beneath
Flashed like a foulsham from its sheath
And many harbour men were stung,
With lashes from his angry tongue,
"What's the delay, in Algoa Bay?"

"Oh! stay, Oh! stay," his captain pressed,
"Go to your bed and have a rest."
The tears welled in his bloodshot eye,
But still he answered with a sigh,
"Must get away, from Algoa Bay."

"Beware the snakes, and big red ants,
Beware the awful immigrants."
This was the captain's last "Good-night!"
A voice replied from Donkins height
"Take me, I pray, from Algoa Bay."

At break of day, as harbour-ward
Went certain men to seek reward,
With many an oath and scarce a prayer--
A voice cried through the startled air,
"What's the delay?" and echoed round the Bay.

(continued)

There in the twilight, cold and grey,
Speechless, but beautiful he lay,
The mariner whose brain gave way
While waiting out in Algoa Bay,
Algoa Bay, Algoa Bay.

Problems in the docks resulted in fourteen ships
waiting out in the Indian Ocean before they could
get into harbour.

"This new monster in our midst,
"That a small child's limbs can twist,
"Deal it now a mortal blow,
"Slay the dragon POLIO!

"Every little help helps a lot,
"And may save a tiny tot;
"Sympathy is not enough,
"Get your hand down -- that's the stuff!"

FAREWELL TO PORT ELIZABETH TRAMS

When Noah stepped forth from the Ark,
In Rink Street, near St. George's Park,
What first met his astounded view?
A P.E. tram, then almost new.

The Greeks of old a battle fought,
Besieging Troy, were gaining nought
Until they tried a battering ram;
Guess what they used? A P.E. tram!

Who knows what those poor trams went through,
With Wellington at Waterloo;
Napoleon was banished far,
Taken a ride -- by a P.E. Car.

For years and years they held the "sway,"
They pitched and tossed like Algoa Bay,
And when they shook, it was not rage,
Nor impish mirth, but sheer old age.

Our memories will linger on,
And after P.E. trams are gone,
We and our grandchildren could see 'em,
If they were kept in some museum.

In 1948 trams were replaced by buses in Port Elizabeth.

III Miscellany

TO THIRSTY MOTORISTS

Do you worship "Speed" the mocker,
Risking death at every trip?
One mistake; a nasty cropper,
Then you're pleading, "Your Worship!"

Have a drink to keep you cheery,
Never think of other lives.
Have another when you're weary,
When you drink the Devil drives.

If you do it fairly regular,
Till your nerves get worse and worse,
Your last trip draws quickly nearer --
In a box inside a hearse.

You don't mean to be a felon,
Motoring gives you such a thirst,
Sell the car, or suck a lemon,
Your only way to "Safety First."

"SUPER SERVICE"

Under a spreading canopy
The filling-station stands;
When I drive in they pounce on me
In nerve-distracting bands,
And try my petrol-cap to free
With eager, oily hands.

The bonnet's flung up with a will,
They grasp a water can,
And pour in water fast, until
It gurgles round the fan;
Good oil upon the engine spill,
Enough to ruin a man.

The windscreen's cleaned, but now looks worse;
Each tyre a boy employs,
They pump the darn things till they burst
With ear-distressing noise,
Then I, who have been known to curse,
Say, "Oh! you naughty boys!"

And children coming home from school,
Look in at my battered door,
Then shout "Hey! mister, there's a pool
Of petrol on the floor!"
Some person strikes a match -- the fool!
I hear a mighty roar . . . .

(continued)

Their fire extinguishers stick fast
So they resort to sand,
And loads on my new car are cast,
Till it's like Summerstrand;
And when they dig it out at last
It's old and secondhand.

Coughing--back firing--spluttering,
Out to the street we go;
I hear attendants muttering,
"No tip, the so-and so!"
Can you blame me for uttering,
"That's Super-service! NO!!!"

"BARGAIN SALE!"

Call me early, mother dear,
I'm going to the sales,
Lay out my bargain-hunting gear,
I'll give you full details.

My crash helmet and boots with spikes,
My shin guards and my gun,
My knobkerrie and assegai,
By jove! there'll be some fun.

I wish I had an armoured car,
Or else a tank with flails,
It's senseless going as you are
To these world-record sales.

Perhaps I'll get a damaged thatch,
And crushed ribs in the press,
But what of that if I can snatch
A bargain--sixpence less!!

So call me early, mother dear,
I must get in the scrum,
And when the 'All Blacks" get this clear,
It's doubtful if they'll come.

Knobkerrie and assegai, Zulu weapons.
All Blacks, famous Rugby team.

HUMBLE FLEA

I am a flea, no pedigree,
But quite a mixer, you'll agree,
A bosom friend, my way I wend
Into the choicest company;
I'm no respecter of persons,
Joining Cohens or McPhersons,
Bringing all unique diversions
With the bite of the humble flea.

With leaps and bounds I go the rounds,
Some duchess may have me for tea;
Ride round the park and make my mark
In all the best society;
A member of the cabinet,
A bishop or a baronet,
Is tattooed where he'd least expect
With the bite of the humble flea.

At bioscopes I know the ropes,
And never fail to get in free;
Fancy panties, fussy aunties,
Are never out of bounds to me;
Working day shift, always nightshift,
On the rump or on the hind-lift,
I import to all my kind gift,
The bite of the humble flea .

There was news in 1948 of a new breed of bigger
fleas. Bioscope, South Africa cinema.

42

SHAKESPEARE AT HOME

One night when Will Shakespeare had worked really hard,
A queer kind of coma came over the bard,
His thoughts left A WINTER'S TALE for a new theme,
The quaintest, the strangest, MIDSUMMER NIGHT'S
DREAM

THE MERCHANT OF VENICE stalked into his room,
And cried "You're a menace, I'll compass your doom;
A full pound of flesh from your body I'll wrench,"
And pinned down the bard on his rude wooden bench.

Now HAMLET, KING LEAR and MACBETH joined the fray,
Determined, it seemed, their creator to slay,
But RICHARD THE SECOND took sides with poor Will,
"Avast, there!," he quoth, "he's immortal--don't kill!"

With MEASURE FOR MEASURE, THE TEMPEST now
raged,

As rough AS YOU LIKE IT, with dozens engaged;
One knave smote OTHELLO to blacken his eye,
'Twas LOVE'S LABOUR LOST--any schoolboy knows why!

Then HENRY THE EIGHTH saw the gleam of long knives,
Found he was surrounded by all his six wives,
Too late now to try THE TAMING OF THE SHREW,
Or ROMEO AND JULIET--his sad fate he knew.

(continued)

The MERRY WIVES OF WINDSOR had eyes full of tears,
JULIUS CAESAR caught Anthony borrowing ears,
This COMEDY OF ERRORS had now reached its height;
When Shakespeare awakened, and so stopped the fight.

"MUCH ADO ABOUT NOTHING," gasped Shakespeare,
relieved,

"But ALL'S WELL THAT ENDS WELL, my life is reprieved;
That's the TWELFTH NIGHT I've wrestled with ink-blooded
men,"

And he slew every one with quick strokes of his pen!

WORLD'S END

The world is now nearing its end,
Or so states an engineer friend,
   So pack up your troubles,
   Or burst them like bubbles,
It surely is time to unbend.

There's no point in going to work
Though this drives the missus berserk,
   Make hay while the sun shines,
   Relax, and make bee lines
From anything tending to irk.

The ice-caps are ready to tip,
And then we shall all have a "trip,"
   That won't be pleasant,
   So live for the present,
And follow my lead--let things slip.

The trouble, of course, lies in this,
When after a deluge of bliss,
   There's no signs of chaos,
   Will this chap repay us,
For prophecies oft go amiss.

Wherever we turn, it appears,
The world will be hung round our ears,
   But if it keeps turning,
   His ears will be burning,
For bringing us pleasure through fears.

An engineer at a conference in 1948,
predicted the world would shortly end.

45

SHOCKING!

Rattle, bang, clatter,
Whatever's the matter --
Is it an explosion
That caused the commotion?
Oh! no, just a miniature 'quake.

But we shouldn't grumble
At this daily rumble --
It certainly keeps us awake.
In life's daily battle
We'll master the rattle
That comes from a miniature 'quake.

A very queer letter
Came in from Melsetter
Requesting "the blasters" to stop,
And a fellow called Charlie,
Who writes from Umtali,
Has asked us to "not let things drop."

It seems that a number
Of folks from the Vumba
Are worried in case they come down,
And find that they've wended
Their way unintended
Right into the centre of town!

The author was caught in an earthquake in Umtali, in Southern Rhodesia. Melsetter and Vumba are towns near Umtali.

WHERE THERE'S SMOKE

It seems my Lady Nicotine
Appears once more upon the scene,
And putting up a dense smoke screen,
Annoys a lot of folk;
When some bad lad at bioscope,
Lights up a pipeful of old rope,
And causes them in gloom to grope,
Their joys go up in smoke.
And yet, the smoker pays his cash,
So wouldn't it be rather rash
For managers their teeth to gnash,
When pipes these fellows stoke;
But surely it is better far,
To hand such chaps a nice cigar,
And have non-smokers saying "Ta!"
Their praise it might evoke.
Now some say all should smoke-abate,
While others talk of a debate,
And thirdly, some would segregate
The heavy-smoking bloke;
But if you give them rope enough
They quickly die of smoker's cough,
A coffin cough that sees 'em off
Victims of habit's yoke.

THE GOOD OLD BREW

Heat the pan on some warm spot,
Place the tea-leaves in the pot,
Pour on water, boiling hot,
And, dear friend, what have you got?
           The good old brew that cheers.

Trickle some into a cup,
Sugar add: with milk fill up,
Try a sip, then take a sup,
Makes you lively as a pup,
           The good old brew that cheers.

It is known in history too,
For the Yankees shouting, "Boo!"
Loads in Boston Harbour threw;
But what hell they later knew
           Without the brew that cheers.

Hitler, full of Caesar's sauce,
London bombed without remorse,
Something beat his great air force,
We know what it was, of course,
           The good old brew that cheers.

ROBBERY

When I switch on the radio
Intent on music's soothing touch,
The wretched things goes "Bo, bo, bo!"
It's swing and boogie, jazz and such.

Some stupid band of ne'er-do-wells
Are banging cans or sticking pigs,
Accompanying a crooner's yells,
To rhythms culled from Kaffir jigs.

I know some people like the stuff
And lap it up with headlong haste,
In fact, they cannot get enough,
And why should I condemn their taste?

If that was where they left the thing
I would not remonstrate at all,
But when good music's turned to swing,
I think a stop we ought to call.

The master tunes of classic stamp
Are wrenched from art's own precious store,
Dressed up with swing and sickening vamp
And plugged at us for evermore.

The menace of these thefts is real;
This gloomy prospect lies before us --
One day the lords of sax appeal
Will swing the Hallelujah Chorus!

OFFICIAL ZEAL

Ah! it's awkward for a copper,
        who is really keen and proper,
For he's bound to come a cropper
        due to his official zeal;
At the first onset of trouble,
        he must get there on the double,
Lest the town's reduced to rubble,
        this is called official zeal.

If a person throws a party,
        it must never get too hearty,
Or he pounces on them smartly
        with a true official zeal,
When some drunks have started singing,
        or their bottles they are flinging,
He must check on their upbringing
        with his swift official zeal.

He must learn what crooks are thinking,
        peering through their wicked blinking,
And arrest them in a winking
        just to show official zeal,
But a copper's ears get hotter,
        when he thinks he's caught a rotter,
And he proves to be a rector,
        that's what curbs official zeal.

(continued)

So a cop in time gets clever,
       and combines Sherlock endeavour
With a spot of "Shall I? Never!,"
       but is that official zeal?
When a person of perfection
       is run in through bad detection,
"This man needed my protection,"
       says the cop with utmost zeal.

MAYOR'S LAMENT

If you please, don't make me Mayor anymore,
I have learnt the post is not a sinecure,
For you rise at early daybreak,
   and make speeches till you've faceache,
If you please, don't make me Mayor anymore.

Every morning there's official work to do,
Such as looking through a new bye-law or two,
One must watch what one is signing,
   and take care who one is fining,
If you please, don't make me Mayor anymore.

At each function, fete or factory affair,
The poor, hard-working Mayor must be there,
Common folk can lounge on sofas,
   and have forty winks, the loafers,
But the Mayor's out in weather foul or fair.

On occasions you must lay foundation stones,
It's such heavy work you ache in all your bones,
Should the building go up twisted,
   It's your fault, it is insisted,
And your name is chiselled there midst moans and groans.

(continued)

Now this tree--planting could be a pleasant task,
But what future has a tree, I humbly ask,
If it isn's dogs that's stopping,
          It's some fool intent on chopping,
Yes! the moral in tree-planting makes me gasp.

When I first donned the Mayoral pinafore,
I had thought my joy would last for evermore,
Till they slipped a chain around me,
          though not lost, it meant they'd found me,
If you please, don't make me Mayor anymore!

MEATY MELODRAMA

I dreamt that I smelt a large juicy steak
With onions and gravy beside,
But when I awoke I soon found my mistake,
It was sausages--SAUSAGES--fried.

Don't go out of your mind, Dad,
Dreams very often come true,
And you know, dear Dad, it would be too sad
If anything happened to you.
Go and tell the butcher your dreams
And as sure as the stars that shine,
Something is going to turn up to-day,
Dear Dad, in the butchery line.

So I went outside, along our street,
Old Sawbones seemed quite pally,
But when I whispered "Any Meat?"
He chased me down an alley.

Come out of the market, Claude,
For the blooming meat has flown,
Come out of the market, Claude,
I fear you will wait alone, alone,
I fear you will wait alone.

(continued)

As I walked along the boulevard
With an independent air,
I heard the folks declare,
"He must be a millionaire,
He's fat, he must be getting meat,
And that is now a rich man's treat,
He's the man who knows a chap in the Black Market."

Take a pair of these meat pies,
And you'll get a rare surprise,
For no meat will pass your lips;
Wait till I shoo off the flies,
From their earthly paradise,
And I'll give you fish and chips;
Our hot dogs are very hot,
I dropped in the pepper-pot;
Or a plate of bouncing peas,
There is energy in these;
You're a dainty man to please,
If you're not satisfied,
If you're not satisfied!

(continued)

Under a spreading chestnut tree,
Another butcher stands,
As I draw near he beckons me,
And kind of flaps his hands,
I dashed across in highest glee,
To make my rash demands.

But he'd only a bird in a gilded cage,
A pitiful sight to see,
It gave a sigh and closed one eye,
Yet it cost me twelve-and-three,
There was sorrow and strife,
When I showed the wife,
She wanted to know its age,
Yes, this beauty was sold,
For a pot of gold,
Just a bird in a gilded cage.

Way down along past Baakens River,
Sadly I roam,
Still hoping for a piece of liver,
To take to the old folks at home.

IV -- Cricket and Other Sports

TIME BOWLS DON

A thrill runs through the watching crowd,
Applause is long, sincere and loud,
The sun now penetrates the cloud,
Don Bradman's at the wicket.
With flashing strokes all round the ground,
To make the score so quickly bound,
Will such another bat be found?
Don Bradman's at the wicket.
A century, a double one,
Perhaps a third before he's done,
And almost every stroke a run,
When Bradman's at the wicket.
With magic in his willow wand,
A symphony of eye and hand
He joins the great immortal band;
Don Bradman's at the wicket.
Alas! he now must say adieu,
Age does what bowlers could not do,
Old Father Time has got one through,
Don Bradman leaves the wicket.
Long may he live to guide the game,
And add more lustre to his name,
The wish of friend and foe the same,
In all the world of cricket.

On the retirement of Don Bradman, one of
the world's greatest batsmen.

TEST MATCH FEVER

What is raging in the town,
Closing every business down?
Smith, Jones, Robinson and Brown,
    All have Test match fever.

Junior clerks fall sick at noon,
Head clerks go off in a swoon,
Even bosses aren't immune,
    Watch that Test match fever.

Young boys dashing to the ground,
Old boys fussing round and round,
Symptoms everywhere abound,
    Contagious Test match fever.

See that crowd inside the Park,
How they stare from noon to dark,
Ah, this thing will leave its mark,
    Loads of Test fever.

Four days of delirium,
Many fight it, most succumb,
Then it leaves one feeling numb,
    Soon cured Test match fever.

Test matches were major cricket matches
that lasted four or five days.

59

THE SPHINX

The wickets fall, they whisper 'rout,'
The Springboks' hope of winning shrinks,
But there's one man they won't get out,
I speak of Bruce, the S.A. Sphinx.

The battles rage, great batsmen fall,
The world is crumbling now, methinks,
One chap meanders through it all,
The Mitchell man, the S.A. Sphinx.

The scorers take a walk round town,
The fieldsmen have their forty winks,
No need to keep the scoring down,
Leave that to Bruce, the modern Sphinx.

He stands there, smile inscrutable,
Come fair, come foul, he never blinks,
Implacable, Immovable,
Impossible, the cricket Sphinx.

If this is cricket, what a game!
It's not a pinch on tiddley-winks!
No monument shall mark its fame
Unless they use the S.A. Sphinx.

Bruce Mitchell maintained his sang froid in a cricket match
between England and South Africa at Port Elizabeth in 1949.

THE DRAGON OF ST. GEORGE'S

There's a breathless hush in St. George's Park,
Jordaan bowls and D. Compton smites,
"Another one out," came a chance remark,
Yes; out of the field, soaring in the heights.
And it's not for the sake of a brand new hat
Or the selfish hope of a season's fame,
Any bowler knows he must beat the bat,
Play up, play up, and play the game!
Jordaan sends down balls of all lengths and kinds,
Drawn from his repertoire of tricks,
And seems to have got Compton in two minds,
Whether to hit him for a four or six!
And it's not for the sake of a brand new hat,
Or the selfish hope of a season's fame,
For the bowler's heard quite enough of that,
Play up, play up, and play the game!
It was in the field he got his revenge,
Jordaan caught one of Compton's hits,
By this catch alone he had made amends
And our Gordon back to the limelight flits.
And it's not for the sake of a brand new hat,
Or the selfish hope of a season's fame,
But G. Jordaan longs for his turn to bat,
Play up, play up, and play the game!

Jordaan and Compton, South African and English cricket
players, 1949

"ALL-IN"

I was a wrestlers referee,
    But now I have resigned,
The heavy duties don't agree
    They're onerous, I find,
Each time the work piles upon me,
    Or kicks me from behind.

This all-in stuff is rather rough,
    They tear themselves apart,
I always thought I was quite tough,
    Until those wrestlers start,
And then I found I'd had enough,
    The work affects my heart.

It's short-arm jabs and Boston crabs,
    Or just a crucifix,
They follow up with furtive grabs,
    Then one or two mule-kicks,
Or press their faces flat as dabs--
    Such naughty little tricks.

Then for a change at shorter range,
    They gouge each other's eyes,
And pull off ears--they do look strange,
    Just like streamlined meat pies,
The sweeper-up quite often faints,
    It's eerie, finding thighs.

(continued)

But when the foes are locked in throes,
  The ref. must intervene,
He has to crawl up through their toes,
  And try to get between.
Just then the fools try fancy throws,
  Do you grasp what I mean?

And if I said "Please use your head,"
  They'd butt about a bit,
But often miss--or so I read,
  For it was me they hit,
So when I came back from the dead,
  I was "all-in," I quit!

A "FISHY" TALE

I went forth with my rod to the Angling Week,
And got a nice spot that fish normally seek,
But for all that I caught with my 5s. wand,
I could have been fishing in St. George's Pond.

I tried all the bait from a fly to a shoe,
Yet none of the fish seemed to know what to do,
Alas! for my visions of tunney and whales,
I saw nothing scaly to send to the scales.

Now I'd heard folk say, "There's more fish in the sea,"
And borrowed a diving-suit down at the quay,
Determined to find what the fishes did keep,
I plunged away down to the watery deep.

When I found my sea-legs in Davy Jones's Land,
I heard the glad sounds of the Steenbrass band,
And there, gathered round on the polished sea-floor,
Were fish gaily dancing and calling for more.

A minuet, stately, and keeping strict time,
Saw sticklebacks escorting skates down the line,
A conger-eel riggled alongside a cod,
But stinging-rays found getting partners a job!

(continued)

64

A "FISHY" TALE (continued)

Then Jock Musselcracker, a gallant young spark,
Requested the pleasure of dainty Miss Shark;
Ah! never before had I witnessed such scenes,
For there were the fish all packed in like sardines.

It seemed 'twas a sort of an Annual Ball,
That lasted a week from morn to nightfall;
Reluctantly leaving the dancing I thought
It isn't the fish, but the men who've been caught!

Colophon

This book was edited and designed by Dr. Alan S. Coulson, M.D., Ph.D.

Typesetting, plates and printing made by E. M. Underwood, Publisher. Paper, the finest obtainable from Zellerbach Paper Company and Fine Binding by Filmer Brothers Bindery San Francisco, California.